UNIT 1

1 LANGUAGE STUDY

I like *and* I'd like

Look at George's answers to the survey. Then complete the questions with *Would you like* **or** *Do you like* **and write appropriate short answers.**

SURVEY

Name _George Murphy_

Give your opinion about the activities below.
Rate them using the following scale:

1 = You do it, and you like it.
2 = You don't do it, but you want to.
3 = You do it sometimes, but you don't like it.
4 = You don't do it, and you don't want to.

READ SCIENCE FICTION *1*

PLAY THE PIANO *3*

COLLECT BUTTERFLIES *2*

TAKE PAINTING LESSONS *4*

STUDY TRIGONOMETRY *4*

PLAY TENNIS *2*

❶ You: ___Do you like___ reading science fiction?

George: ___Yes, I do___. I love it!

❷ You: _____ playing the piano?

George: _____. I think it's boring.

❸ You: _____ to collect butterflies?

George: _____. I think it would be fun.

❹ You: _____ to take painting lessons?

George: _____. I'm not very artistic.

❺ You: _____ to study trigonometry?

George: _____. Math has never been my favorite subject.

❻ You: _____ to play tennis?

George: _____. Maybe I'll take lessons next summer.

2 *WHAT ABOUT YOU?*

**Look at the activities in the survey. Write about what you like
or don't like doing, and about what you would or wouldn't like to do.**

❶ _____

❷ _____

❸ _____

❹ _____

❺ _____

❻ _____

3 *LANGUAGE STUDY*

The Present Perfect Progressive, the Present Progressive, and the Simple Past

A **Read the newspaper article. Then complete the questions the reporter asked Mario,
using the Present Perfect Progressive, the Present Progressive, or the Simple Past.
Then choose the correct answer.**

Opera Star to Perform

Mario Salerno, one of the world's best-loved opera stars, arrived in Vienna today for a two-week visit. This is the last stop on his five-month tour of Europe. In addition to his opera performances, Mario will appear with other celebrities tomorrow evening in a special benefit show for children with heart disease.

Mario started singing professionally ten years ago, but before that he worked as a piano teacher in a small college for about five years. When asked about his memories of those years, Mario said, "I made some really good friends when I was there, and I still write to many of my students." In fact, Mario's best student accompanies him on all his trips. Welcome to Vienna, Mrs. Salerno!

VIENNA, MAY 1, 1990

❶ Reporter: How long ___*are you staying*___ (*stay*) in Vienna?

    Mario: **a** For three weeks.
                  b Until May 15th.
                  c Last week.

❷ Reporter: How long _____ (*travel*) around Europe?

    Mario: **a** For five years.
                  b For almost five months.
                  c For two weeks.

❸ Reporter: How long _____ (*sing*) professionally?

    Mario: **a** Since 1985.
                  b Since 1980.
                  c For five years.

❹ Reporter: How long _____ (*work*) as a piano teacher?

    Mario: **a** At least a month.
                  b For five years.
                  c Until May.

❺ Reporter: How long _____ (*write*) to your students?

    Mario: **a** Since I was a piano teacher.
                  b Since I went to college.
                  c For ten years.

B Olivia Patterson, the famous ballet dancer, will also perform in the benefit show on May 2nd. Look at her time line. Then write a short article about her, in the space provided on the next page. Use the article about Mario as a model.

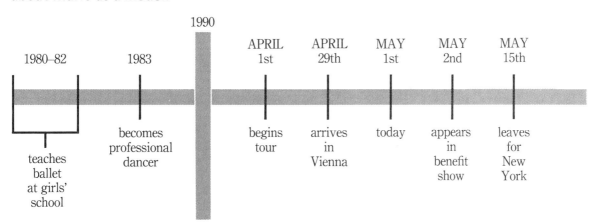

_____

_____

_____

_____

_____

_____

_____

4 _WHAT ABOUT YOU?_

Make your own time line. Then write a short paragraph using that information.

_____

_____

_____

_____

5 _VOCABULARY_

A   **Look at page 5 of your textbook. Find a word or phrase in the text, "A Dead Film About a Dead Actor," that means the same or almost the same as the words and phrases below.**

1 to start   _____

2 attraction, charm _____

3 doesn't have   _____

4 stayed   _____

5 a fixed idea   _____

6 correct, precise   _____

B **Now look at the other two texts on page 5 of your textbook. Complete the chart with a word or phrase that means the same or almost the same as the words and phrases below.**

1 ask for   _____

2 father   _____

3 kid   _____

4 he would   _____

5 however   _____

6 conversing   _____

7 unaccompanied   _____

8 October 16th   _____

One word in each of the pairs is more informal or more colloquial than the other. Decide which one it is and circle it.

6 *LANGUAGE STUDY*

Verb + do, to do, *or* doing

A **Complete the conversation with *do, to do*, or *doing*.**

A: Do you enjoy

¹ _____ the

housework, Susan?

B: No, I hate it. I think it's really boring. When I was a child my mother

always made me ² _____ things around the house. I

especially hated ³ _____ the dishes. I kept

⁴ _____ a bad job, but she never said anything. I wanted

her to say, "Stop ⁵ _____ the dishes, and go watch TV."

She never did. One year, I suggested ⁶ _____ something

special for Mom's birthday. I had a serious talk with my father. I

promised ⁷ _____ my homework every night and to try

⁸ _____ better in school. The next day we went out and

bought Mom the perfect gift ... a beautiful new dishwasher. That was

one of the happiest days of my life.

B Refer to the conversation and complete the sentences with the words below.

(to) (at) (in) (with)

❶ Susan wasn't good _____ washing the dishes.

❷ She was more interested _____ watching TV.

❸ She looked forward _____ buying a dishwasher for her mother.

❹ Now Susan is bored _____ doing all kinds of housework.

7 WHAT ABOUT YOU?

**Complete each question with the correct form of one of
the verbs. Then answer the question.**

(watch) (get up) (live) (learn) (do) (sleep) (go) (eat)

❶ What would you like _____ for dinner tonight?

_____

❷ Do you prefer _____ early or late?

_____

❸ Where do you plan _____ for your next vacation?

_____

❹ Are you interested in _____ another foreign language?

_____

❺ What are you looking forward to _____ next weekend?

_____

❻ Do you ever think about _____ in another country?

_____

❼ Do you ever stop _____ TV because you don't like the program?

_____

❽ How many hours do you need _____ every night?

_____

8 *LANGUAGE STUDY*

The Future with the Present Progressive

A We can use the Present Progressive instead of *going to* or *will* to talk about future actions that can be definitely planned or arranged.
Find three sentences that can be used in the Present Progressive and rewrite them.

1 It's going to rain tomorrow.

2 Mary's going to go shopping.

3 One of Mary's friends is going to go with her.

4 She'll borrow her brother's car because he isn't going to use it.

5 She saw some pretty boots, but she doesn't know if they'll fit.

6 She's sure they'll have a good time.

_____

_____

_____

B Complete the sentences below with the Present Progressive if possible. If not, use *going to* or *will*.

1 John and Susan (*go*) _____ to a baseball game this weekend.

2 Do you think it (*rain*) _____ during the night?

3 I (*get*) _____ a headache if I drink too much champagne at the party.

4 The plant (*die*) _____ if you don't water it.

5 The class (*take*) _____ a trip at the end of the semester.

6 Jane (*visit*) _____ her cousin when she finishes work.

7 My sister (*get married*) _____ in two weeks.

8 Joe (*paint*) _____ the house in the spring.

9 Shh! The movie (*start*) _____ in a few minutes!

10 You (*fall*) _____ if you're not careful.

9 *WRITING*

Write a conversation between you and a friend. It's Friday afternoon and you're telling each other about your plans for the weekend. Discuss the details and decide to do something together.

Use some of these words and phrases:

think about   Would you like   prefer   be interested in

going to   be ...ing

UNIT 2

1 LANGUAGE STUDY
Tag Questions

A   Read the conversation. Then add tag questions using the words below.

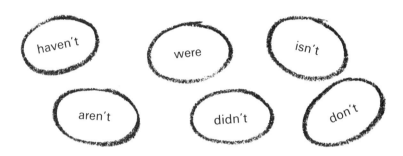

John: Hello. You're new at the office, [1] _____?

Barbara: Yes, as a matter of fact, I am. I started working here last week. You work in the Accounting

          Department, [2] _____?

John: Yes, I do. You know, you look very familiar. I think we've met before, [3] _____?

Barbara: I don't think so. I've only been in town for three weeks.

John: Where are you from?

Barbara: Los Angeles.

John: Let's see. I was in Los Angeles about two years ago. You weren't taking a course at UCLA,

          [4] _____?

Barbara: Yes! That's right. I remember! We had the same teacher for marketing, [5] _____?

John: Of course! That's where we met. It's a small world, [6] _____?

B   Now write a response to each of the comments in an appropriate way to show interest on the part of the speaker. Use a tag question.

❶   Barbara: Our course at UCLA was really interesting.

    John: *It really was, wasn't it ?*

❷   John: We sure had a lot of homework.

    Barbara: _____

❸   John: I enjoyed living in Los Angeles.

    Barbara: _____

❹   Barbara: I was lucky to get a job here.

    John: _____

❺   Barbara: I find the work difficult, but challenging.

    John: _____

❻   John: I think the company is having a picnic on the 4th of July.

    Barbara: _____

2 LANGUAGE STUDY

Other Ways to Keep the Conversation Going

Read the four conversations. Add an additional question to each one to keep it going.

❶   A: Would you like to go to a Chinese restaurant?
    B: Yeah! I'd love to.

    A: _____ ?

❷   A: Have you ever gone on a boat trip?
    B: No, I haven't. But I'd really like to.

    A: _____ ?

❸   A: Could you tell me about the new sports club?
    B: Sure. What would you like to know?

    A: _____ ?

❹   A: You speak English very well. How long have you been studying?
    B: Just for a few months, but I really enjoy my classes.

    A: _____ ?

3 LANGUAGE STUDY

Asking People to Do Things

Match each request with the correct picture. Then circle the letter of the most appropriate answer.

❶ "Sit down and be quiet."
  a "Thanks, Mom."   **b** "OK."

❷ "Will you lend me your dictionary?"
  a "It would be an honor."   **b** "Sure."

❸ "North Bus Terminal, please. As fast as you can."
  a "Yes, ma'am."   **b** "Yes, sir."

❹ "Won't you sit down, please."
  a "Thank you."   **b** "Thanks."

❺ "Could you tell me where to find the Spanish–English dictionaries, please?"
  a "Yeah. They're over on that table in the corner."
  b "Yes, sir. They're on the second shelf."

❻ Excuse me. Would you mind telling me where the American Express Office is?"
  a "I'm sorry. I'm really not sure."   **b** "I have no idea."

4 LANGUAGE STUDY
Making Comparisons

Add an appropriate word to complete each comparison.

1 The old man had a soft white beard, like _____*cotton*_____.

2 Her _____ had a wonderful, sweet fragrance, just like spring flowers.

3 He wasn't very handsome. He had big _____, just like an elephant.

4 The _____ was really comfortable, just like old shoes.

5 Her _____ were very cold, just like ice.

6 The athlete ran very fast, like _____.

7 She had beautiful white teeth, like _____.

8 The bread the old man was eating was hard, like _____.

5 *LANGUAGE STUDY*

The Simple Past or the Present Perfect

A   Read about Laura. Then match the sentences 1–6 with the phrases a–f to make six logical sentences.

Eating Out

Laura started a new job three weeks ago and she's been too busy to go home for lunch. Eating out every day has made Laura gain ten pounds.

<u>b</u>	❶ Laura hasn't had time to cook lunch	**a** twice already.
_____	❷ She's put on a lot of weight	**b** for almost three weeks.
_____	❸ She decided to start a diet	**c** three days ago and she's going to follow it.
_____	❹ She bought some diet pills,	**d** but she hasn't taken them yet.
_____	❺ She's been to the gym	**e** since she started eating out.
_____	❻ She hasn't noticed any difference	**f** since she started eating less.

B Now complete Laura's letter to her Aunt Liz with the correct form of the verb in parentheses. Use the Simple Past or the Present Perfect.

Dear Aunt Liz,

Sorry for not writing sooner! How's everybody? I really like my new job, but I have long hours and a lot of work. I have to eat out a lot at lunchtime, and as you can probably guess, I ¹(gain)_____ a lot of weight since I arrived. I ²(be)_____ on a diet for a few weeks now, but I'm going to have to stop soon. It's really expensive! Last week I ³(spend)_____ a lot of money on fresh fruit and vegetables. I ⁴(decide)_____ to join a gym and I ⁵(go)_____ every day for the last couple of weeks. That's very expensive, too.

Besides my weight, everything else is fine. I ⁶(find)_____ a nice apartment the day after I arrived. I ⁷(meet)_____ some nice people since I started work. As a matter of fact, last night a group of us ⁸(go)_____ to the opera house together. We ⁹(see)_____ "Madame Butterfly." It was fantastic! So, as you can see, I ¹⁰(be)_____ very busy.

I ¹¹(not write)_____ to Aunt Mary and Uncle Bob yet. Tell them I'm fine, and that I'll write soon.

Love,
Laura

6 LANGUAGE STUDY

Two-Word Verbs

A   Match each two-word verb with the correct definition.

_____	❶ give up	**a**	take care of
_____	❷ come back	**b**	return
_____	❸ look out	**c**	continue
_____	❹ go on	**d**	stop
_____	❺ look after	**e**	use a book to find information
_____	❻ run into	**f**	complete (a form)
_____	❼ fill in / out	**g**	meet unexpectedly
_____	❽ look up	**h**	be careful

B   Now complete the story with the following two-word verbs. Be sure to use the correct tense.

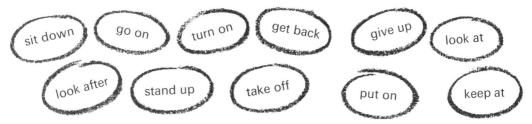

sit down   go on   turn on   get back   give up   look at

look after   stand up   take off   put on   keep at

To Smoke or Not to Smoke?

John ¹ _____ nervously, thanked Dr.Brady and left the hospital. It was one o'clock when

John ² _____ to his office. He had a strange expression on his face and

³ _____ repeating the same sentence over and over, "I can do it! I can do it!" John had made

up his mind; he was going to quit smoking. ⁴ _____ cigarettes wasn't going to be easy. He

⁵ _____ at his desk and ⁶_____ the calendar. It was March 18th, his 40th

birthday, and he felt like an old man. "I'm going to ⁷_____ some weight," he thought. "But

I'm going to ⁸ _____ it! After all, I have to ⁹ _____ my health." That day

John couldn't concentrate. Everything reminded him of smoking. He ¹⁰ _____ his jacket ...

an empty pack of cigarettes fell to the floor. He ¹¹ _____ the radio ... an ad for a mild new cigarette. He opened the newspaper … cigarette lighters on sale. It was six o'clock. Everybody was leaving the office. It was time to go home. Suddenly John felt good. "My first day at the office without smoking," he thought. "I can do it! I can do it!"

C   The two-word verbs in four of the sentences in "To Smoke or Not to Smoke?" can be separated. Find those four sentences and write them in a different way.

❶ _____

_____

❷ _____

_____

❸ _____

_____

❹ _____

_____

7 *VOCABULARY*

Can you figure out these relationships?

Family Puzzle

❶ Your mother's sister's daughter is your _____.

❷ Your niece's brother is your _____.

❸ Your grandmother's son's wife is your _____.

or your _____.

❹ Your husband's sister's brother is your _____.

❺ Your daughter's brother's wife is your _____.

❻ Your cousin's father's father is your _____.

8 *WRITING*

**Look at the biography Paul wrote about his uncle. His
teacher has circled the mistakes. Can you correct them?**

My uncle Joe is a (man tall and slim.)He's about 60 years old. He looks a lot older because his hair is

completely white, like(fire.)He(has been born)in a small town in New Jersey, and has lived there all his life.

Every June, a few weeks before school is out, he calls and asks, "You're coming to visit this summer,(don't)

you?" Then he(goes at)telling me about the plans he has(make)for us. I guess Uncle Joe is kind of lonely. Aunt

Sarah has been dead(since)ten years now and they never had any children of their own. They(looked me after)

a lot when I was a little boy and we lived in New Jersey.

Uncle Joe is good at almost everything. He's an excellent cook; I always(take on)two or three pounds when

I'm there. He knows a lot about animals. He loves birds and he(stands up)early every day to go birdwatching.

We never(get on)the television when I'm there. We're outside all day until the sun(goes up.)Last year I(have)

learned how to fish. I(went)with some friends three times this year, but I'm still not as good as Uncle Joe. I

guess I'm really lucky to have an uncle like Uncle Joe,(amn't I?)

UNIT 3

LANGUAGE STUDY

The Past Progressive and the Simple Past

A **Complete the three paragraphs about famous people by using the verbs in the correct tense.**

Charlie Chaplin [1] (*appear*) _____ on stage for the first

time when he [2] (*be*) _____ only five years old. His

mother [3] (*perform*) _____ when all of a sudden she

[4] (*lose*) _____ her voice. She couldn't continue so

Charlie Chaplin [5] (*walk*) _____ out on stage and

[6] (*sing*) _____ a song for the audience.

An earthquake [7] (*hit*) _____ the city of San Francisco

in 1906. Enrico Caruso [8] (*sing*) _____ at the time.

Caruso [9] (*run*) _____ to his dressing room and

[10] (*save*) _____ one possession: an autographed

photograph of Theodore Roosevelt, the U.S. president at that time.

In 1903 the Wright brothers [11] (*have*) _____ an

accident when they [12] (*fly*) _____ in their small

wooden plane. It [13] (*be*) _____ a very windy day, and

the plane was destroyed. The two brothers [14] (*not lose*) _____

_____ hope. They [15] (*pick up*) _____

all the broken pieces of the airplane that they could find, [16] (*pack up*)

_____ them _____, and [17] (*send*

back) _____ them _____ home.

18

B Look at the three paragraphs and answer the questions.

1 What was Charlie Chaplin's mother doing when she lost her voice?

_____

2 What did Charlie Chaplin do when his mother lost her voice?

_____

3 What was Caruso doing when the earthquake hit?

_____

4 What did Caruso do when the earthquake hit?

_____

5 What were the Wright brothers doing when they had their accident?

_____

6 What did the Wright brothers do when they had their accident?

_____

C Complete the sentences with the Simple Past or the Past Progressive.

1 Mr. Ryan (*read*) _____ the newspaper when he smelled something burning.

2 When he saw the smoke, he (*jump*) _____ up from his seat.

3 He (*walk*) _____ toward the kitchen when he was blinded by smoke.

4 When he realized the kitchen was on fire, he (*call*) _____ the fire department.

5 His hands (*shake*) _____ when he picked up the phone.

6 He (*give*) _____ his address and then he ran outside.

7 He (*wait*) _____ on the sidewalk, when he heard the siren.

8 He (*feel*) _____ relieved when he saw the fire truck.

9 The firefighters (*put out*) _____ the fire and then they (*leave*) _____.

2 LANGUAGE STUDY

Past Progressive with while

John and Margaret have very different work schedules. She works days and he works nights. Look at the chart and then make sentences about what they were doing at the same time yesterday.

Margaret	John
8:00 a.m. – get ready for work	8:00 a.m. – drive home from work
8:30–9:00 – read the morning paper	8:30–9:00 – get ready for bed
9:00–5:00 – work	9:00–5:00 – sleep
5:00–6:00 – have dinner	5:00–6:00 – have lunch
6:00–7:00 – go shopping	6:00–7:00 – play tennis
8:00–9:00 – watch TV	8:00–9:00 – read the evening paper
10:00–11:00 – listen to music	10:00–11:00 – eat dinner
12:00 – go to bed	12:00 – go to work

➊ *While Margaret was getting ready for work, John was driving home from work.*

➋ _____

➌ _____

➍ _____

➎ _____

➏ _____

➐ _____

➑ _____

3 WHAT ABOUT YOU?

1 What were you doing yesterday while Margaret was having dinner?

_____

2 What were you doing yesterday while John was reading the evening paper?

_____

4 VOCABULARY

Complete the chart.

VERB	NOUN	VERB	NOUN
1 live	_life_	**7** exist	_____
2 _____	death	**8** _____	performance
3 see	_____	**9** _____	refusal
4 _____	passage	**10** excite	_____
5 succeed	_____	**11** please	_____
6 _____	mixture	**12** compete	_____

5 VOCABULARY

A One word in each category does not belong there. Circle it and then add another word that belongs to that category. If necessary look at the chart on page 24 of your textbook for help.

1 dyed / curly / fat / dark _____

2 overweight / short / tall / elegant _____

3 young / reserved / generous / friendly _____

4 white / green / hazel / blue _____

5 pretty / attractive / bald / casually dressed _____

6 shy / elegant / rude / conceited _____

B   Fill in each blank with an appropriate word.

Patrick is very different from his three brothers both in personality and

looks. His brothers are all very outgoing, but Patrick is quite

[1] _____ and [2] _____. Patrick is a

[3] _____ boy and because of that he doesn't laugh

often. Patrick's eyesight isn't very good, and he wears

[4] _____ most of the time. His brothers are very thin,

but he tends to eat a little too much and he's always a few pounds

[5] _____. Patrick is the only one in his family with

[6] _____ hair; the others all have brown or black hair.

Patrick's just starting to grow a [7] _____ and a

[8] _____, and they're [9] _____ too. His

eyes are as [10] _____ as the sky, and everybody says

Patrick is an [11] _____ boy although he's not as

handsome as his brothers.

6 LANGUAGE STUDY

Idioms that Use Parts of the Body

A   Complete the following expressions with a part of the body. Then use the expressions in the conversation making any necessary changes.

to have your _____ in the right place

to get cold _____

to be up to your _____ in work

to keep your _____ crossed

to get something off your _____

Pat: Are you OK, Sam? You look a little worried or nervous.

Sam: Well, I wanted to tell you something, but I really don't know if I should.

Pat: Come on, Sam [1] _____! What is it?

Sam: Well, you know, I was going to ask my boss for a raise, but I didn't. I just couldn't.

Pat: Why not? You [2] _____ ever since you started at that

 office.

Sam: Yeah! I know that, and you know that! I guess [3] _____.

 I'll ask for the raise tomorrow.

Pat: Well, I'll [4] _____! I'm sure Mr. Grove will say "yes." He's

 a hard man to work for, but he [5] _____.

B Match each idiomatic expression with the correct meaning.

_____ **1** to keep an eye on

_____ **2** to have a good ear

_____ **3** to stick your neck out

_____ **4** to talk behind someone's back

_____ **5** to keep your nose out of something

_____ **6** to pull someone's leg

_____ **7** to break someone's heart

_____ **8** to lose your head

a to make someone sad

b to take a risk

c to watch carefully

d to have a special ability to distinguish sounds

e to joke with someone

f to lose control

g to stop interfering

h to say things about another person

C Now use the idiomatic expressions to complete the sentences.

1 They say that people who _____ for music usually speak

 foreign languages very well.

2 Don't be silly. _____ to help John. He's never done

 anything for you.

3 _____ the baby for a few minutes while I take a shower?

4 Did you read the story about the little girl who needs a heart transplant? It just _____

_____ .

5 If Liz doesn't stop _____ , I'm going to get mad. Why

does she always have to talk about everyone?

6 Be calm! _____ . Think about it carefully. Don't make a

decision you'll be sorry about later.

7 You drive me crazy. You're always telling me what to do! Can't you _____

_____ ?

8 I really thought Tom was serious when he told me he was moving to Hawaii, but he

_____ .

---

7 *WHAT ABOUT YOU?*

1 When would you stick your neck out to help another person?

_____

2 What kinds of situations make you lose your head?

_____

3 Has anybody ever talked about you behind your back?
What did you do?

_____

4 Have you ever gotten cold feet?

_____

5 When was the last time you pulled someone's leg?
What did you do?

_____

8 WRITING

Use the cues to complete the letter.

Dear Susie,

Guess what? I wanted you to be the first to know ... I'm getting married in June! Can you believe it! We're both (*describe how you feel*) _____. My fiancé(e)'s name is (*invent a name*) _____. I met _____ last summer (*say where you met him or her*) _____. (*say what you were doing when you saw him/her for the first time*) _____ when I saw _____ for the first time. (*say what he/she was doing*) _____ with some friends. That same evening I ran into _____ again (*say where*) _____. We started to talk and found out we had a lot in common. Isn't that amazing? I'm sure you'll really like _____ when you meet him/her. He/She's (*describe your fiancé(e)'s personality*) _____. He/She looks a little like (*say who he/she looks like*) _____; he/she's (*mention height*) _____ and he/she (*mention general physical appearance*) _____. Anyway, I can't wait for you two to meet. Let me know when you're planning to be in town and the three of us can get together for dinner.

Call me soon.

Love,

(*your name*) _____

UNIT 4

1 LANGUAGE STUDY

The Past with used to

A   Match sentences with similar meanings.

_____ ❶ I used to go to work by bus.

_____ ❷ I usually go to work by bus.

_____ ❸ Did you use to live near your work?

_____ ❹ Do you live near your work?

_____ ❺ I didn't use to be late for work.

_____ ❻ I'm not usually late for work.

a Most of the time I take the bus to work.

b I'm almost never late for work.

c I was never late for work before.

d Is your work near your house?

e Did you live near your work before you moved?

f Before I bought a car, I went to work by bus.

B   Complete the conversations with _used to_ and an appropriate verb.

❶ A: Has Mary always had red hair?

B: Oh, no. She __*used to have*_____ blond hair, but I think

she's much more attractive now.

A: It's too bad she's so thin. Has she been on a diet?

B: I think so. She _____ overweight.

❷ A: Public transportation has really gone up in price, hasn't it?

B: It sure has. It _____ a lot cheaper.

A: John's smart. He walks to work every day, doesn't he?

B: Just since he moved. He _____ the train, but he lives

a lot closer now.

❸ A: The Smiths' yard always looks so nice. Do they take care of it themselves?

   B: Their son does. They _____ a gardener, but

      he retired last year.

   A: I didn't know they had a son.

   B: Oh, yeah! He _____ to school with my

      daughter. He must be about 17, too.

❹ A: I'm looking for a new dentist for the boys. Can you recommend one?

   B: Let's see. I _____ my kids

      to Dr. Thomson. He was great! But he's moved to Florida.

      His son has taken over his practice.

   A: Do you have his telephone number?

   B: Let's see. I _____ it by heart, but

      I've forgotten it. I'll have to check in my address book.

**C Now look at the conversations again, and complete these sentences
with *used to* or *didn't use to*.**

❶ Mary _____ have red hair.

❷ Public transportation _____ be less

   expensive.

❸ John _____ live close to his work.

❹ The Smiths never _____ take care of their yard

   themselves.

❺ Dr. Thomson _____ live in Florida.

D Look at the objects in the picture. Harry has gotten or bought all of these things for the first time this year. Write sentences about things that Harry didn't use to do.

1 He *didn't use to drive.*

2 _____

3 _____

4 _____

5 _____

2 WHAT ABOUT YOU?

When you were a child ...

1 What kind of food did you use to like?

_____

2 What kind of books did you use to read?

_____

3 What did you use to do on Saturday afternoons?

_____

4 What did you use to do for your summer vacations?

_____

5 What time did you use to get up?

_____

6 What time did you use to go to bed?

_____

3 LANGUAGE STUDY

Reflexive and Reciprocal Pronouns

Complete the conversation with

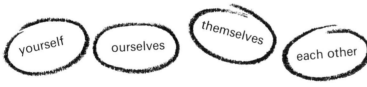

yourself   ourselves   themselves   each other

Jack: How's your new roommate?

Ed: He's very nice. We really didn't know [1] _____

very well before, but now we're good friends. Fred is a great guy!

Jack: I'm glad to hear that. By the way, I like your furniture.

Was it all here when you moved in?

Ed: Oh, no. We made all of it [2] _____. It wasn't easy,

but it was fun. It just takes practice. Here. Try this chair. Fred

and his brother made this one [3] _____. Sit down

and make [4] _____ at home. Have some cookies.

Jack: These are delicious! Did you make them [5] _____?

Ed: Are you kidding? I'm terrible in the kitchen. We eat mostly sandwiches

and pizza. My mother made the cookies, and brought them over

yesterday.

Jack: Well, I hate to eat and run, but I really have to go.

Ed: Come on. Wait just a few minutes. Fred will be back at seven

o'clock. I really want you two to meet [6] _____.

Jack: OK. I'll wait a while. Could you do me a favor and ask your mother

for her cookie recipe? I'd love to try making some.

Ed: Sure. She calls them Molly and Maude's Nut Cookies. She and her

sister invented the recipe [7] _____. Oh, look.

Here's Fred now.

4 LANGUAGE STUDY

Only a little *and* only a few

A **Complete the sentences with *only a little* or *only a few*, and then number them in the correct order.**

_____ After you mix those ingredients, you add _____ nuts.

_____ Here's the recipe for Molly and Maude's Nut Cookies.

_____ Put the cookies in the oven, but for _____

minutes or they'll get hard.

_____ Finally, you mix in some milk, but _____ or

the cookies will be wet inside.

_____ You don't need many ingredients: _____ sugar, butter, and flour.

_____ Take the cookies out of the oven, let them cool, and in _____

while they're ready to eat.

B **Rewrite each sentence using *only a little*.**

❶ I have only a few dollars in the bank.

  <u>I have only a little money in the bank.</u>

❷ They sold only a few bottles of wine.

  _____

❸ He speaks only a few words of German.

  _____

❹ I have only a few free hours every day.

  _____

❺ I like only a few drops of milk in my coffee.

  _____

❻ We have only a few things in the refrigerator.

  _____

5 LANGUAGE STUDY

Using like *and* prefer

A Match sentences with similar meanings.

_____ ❶ John prefers meat to fish.

_____ ❷ John used to prefer eating fish to meat.

_____ ❸ John likes beer more than wine.

_____ ❹ John used to like wine more than beer.

a John likes meat more than fish.

b John prefers beer to wine.

c John liked fish more than meat.

d John preferred drinking wine to drinking beer.

B Interpret the chart about John's preferences. Complete the sentences with *like* or *prefer* and words from the chart. Include an appropriate verb when necessary.

✔ winter sports	☐ summer sports
✔ team sports	☐ individual sports
✔ theater	☐ movies
✔ novels	☐ magazines
☐ concerts	✔ discos
✔ science museums	☐ art museums
☐ TV news programs	✔ TV sports programs

❶ John ___*likes winter sports*___ more than summer sports.

❷ John _____ to individual sports.

❷ John _____ more than going to the movies.

❹ John _____ to reading magazines.

❺ John _____ more than going to concerts.

❻ John _____ to art museums.

❼ John _____ more than TV news programs.

6 WHAT ABOUT YOU?

Answer with complete sentences about yourself.

❶ Which do you prefer, a light breakfast or a big breakfast?

_____

❷ Which do you like more, staying home on weekends or going out?

_____

❸ Which did you prefer when you were a child, eating cookies and cake or eating meat?

_____

❹ Which did you like more when you were a child, watching TV or playing outside?

_____

7 LANGUAGE STUDY

Comparing Things with more/less/fewer ... than

Look at the two job announcements. Then complete the sentences with

Care Insurance Co.

We need a part-time
English–Spanish bilingual secretary.

● Morning hours

● $15,000 starting salary

● 2 weeks vacation

ESA Sales

This is your opportunity!
We offer:
3 full-time positions for salespeople.
Must be willing to travel.
● Free company car
● $20,000 salary + commissions
● Free medical care
● 1 month vacation

❶ ESA pays _____ money than Care Insurance.

❷ Care Insurance gives _____ benefits than ESA Sales.

❸ Employees at Care Insurance get _____ vacation.

❹ The job as salesperson requires _____ hours of work.

❺ The person hired by Care Insurance will have to work _____ hours.

8 WRITING

Imagine that you are a new employee at ESA Sales or Care Insurance Co.
Write a letter to a friend saying:

1 Where you saw the job ad.

2 When you started work.

3 What you like most about the job.

4 Why you prefer this job to your previous job.

5 How it compares to your previous job (salary, hours, vacation, benefits).

UNIT 5

1 LANGUAGE STUDY
The Passive Voice

A   Read the sentences and underline the correct verb.

1 Rice (*eats* / *is eaten*) with chopsticks in China, but in Western countries most people (*are eaten* / *eat*) rice with a fork.

2 In some countries sandwiches (*are eaten* / *eat*) with a fork and a knife; in other countries people (*use* / *are used*) their hands.

3 More milk (*is drunk* / *drinks*) in Canada than in Germany, but the Irish (*drink* / *are drunk*) more milk than the Canadians.

4 Potatoes (*brought* / *were brought*) to Europe in the sixteenth century, but the Europeans (*weren't accepted* / *didn't accept*) them right away.

B   Complete the sentences with the words in parentheses and the Passive Voice.

American supermarkets or grocery stores are the shopper's dream. Almost any kind of food imaginable [1](*can* / *find*) _____**can be found**_____ there. Years ago these stores closed on Sundays and at night, but nowadays shoppers [2](*can* / *see*) _____ carrying brown paper bags at any time of day or night. You don't even need money to go shopping; paying by check or credit card [3](*permit*) _____ _____ in most supermarkets. Big shopping carts [4](*use*) _____ to make shopping easier. The different foods [5](*arrange*) _____ attractively in wide aisles. This makes for easy shopping. Many other products besides food [6](*can* / *find*) _____ in the supermarket. All kinds of cleaning supplies, household gadgets, and even toys or plants [7](*sell*) _____ _____ there too. Special discount coupons [8](*include*) _____ in most newspapers, and these [9](*collect*) _____ by the "good" shopper. By using these coupons a lot of money [10](*can* / *save*) _____ on the weekly shopping.

2 *WHAT ABOUT YOU?*

1 On what days and at what times are grocery stores open in your country?

_____

2 Are shopping carts provided for the shoppers?

_____

3 Can other things besides food be bought? If so, what?

_____

3 *VOCABULARY*

Complete the menu with the following words. Use each word only once.

fried   baked   grilled   boiled   roasted

Randy's Restaurant

All our meals are served with our own freshly

¹_____ bread.

Gourmet garden salad: Lettuce, tomato, tuna fish, carrots, olives,

² hard-_____ eggs seasoned with mild olive oil.

Randy's special ³_____ **steak:** cooked to your taste on our

charcoal barbecue.

Heavenly oven lamb: Baby leg of lamb, ⁴_____ daily in our

wood oven and served with fresh green peas and potatoes.

Fisherman's plate: fresh fish dipped in flour and then ⁵_____

in hot oil, served with french fries.

---

4 *LANGUAGE STUDY*

Adjectives Ending in –ed *and* –ing

**A   Match each person or situation with an appropriate adjective.
Use each adjective only once.**

_____ **1** a three-hour math class

_____ **2** the sidewalk on a hot summer day

_____ **3** a child after five hours at the beach

_____ **4** a woman watching a terrible movie for the

second time

_____ **5** a tourist accused of robbery in a foreign

country

_____ **6** an earthquake, a tornado, or a terrible storm

a burning
b boring
c frightened
d burned
e bored
f frightening

**B   Complete the conversations by making adjectives
from the verbs in parentheses.**

1 A: I was really (*disappoint*) _____ in our team

yesterday. I was sure they were going to win.

B: You're right! It was a very (*disappoint*) _____

game. As a matter of fact, I was so (*bore*) _____

that I left before the game ended. Did anything (*excite*) _____

happen in the last ten minutes?

A: Are you kidding? I felt very (*embarrass*) _____

for our team. They were so (*exhaust*) _____ by the end

of the game that they couldn't even run. The final score was 7–0.

B: Oh, no! It should be (*interest*) _____ to

see what happens next Saturday. I hope they do better.

2 A: Did you read the (*amuse*) _____ story in the paper

yesterday about the man who thought he saw a UFO?

B: No. Why was it so funny?

A: Well, this old man woke up in the middle of the night because he heard a strange noise. He was

really (*frighten*) _____, but he was able to get up and look

out the window.

B: Is that when he saw the UFO?

A: Well, he saw what he called a (*terrify*) _____

bright light coming towards him from the distance. He felt

(*surprise*) _____ and (*confuse*) _____.

He said, "I didn't know what to do! I started to panic."

B: Then what happened?

A: He called the police department and the fire department and in five

minutes they were all there. The poor man was really (*embarrass*) _____!

When they all walked over to the spot where the light was coming from, they found a movie

director and his team shooting a scene for a new movie called "A Visitor from Another Dimension."

5 WHAT ABOUT YOU?

Give your opinion by completing each sentence with an appropriate adjective ending in –ed or –ing.

1 Rainy days are _____ .

2 Books about love and romance are _____ .

3 Students who do well on a test usually feel _____ .

4 Spy and adventure movies are _____ .

5 Going shopping is _____ .

6 Seeing your favorite team lose makes you feel _____ .

6 *LANGUAGE STUDY*

I'd rather (not) ... *and* I'd prefer (not) ...

Complete each conversation with

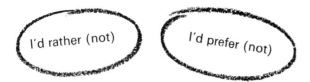

I'd rather (not)   I'd prefer (not)

Conversation 1

A: Would you like a cup of coffee?

B: No thanks, _____ to have a cup of tea.

A: What about a piece of chocolate cake?

B: That sounds delicious, but _____ eat anything

now. Bob's invited me out to an early dinner tonight.

Conversation 2

A: Would you like to try a slice of one of our homemade pies?

B: I'd love to, but I've eaten so much. I think _____

get one to take out. Then I can enjoy it later on. That's

possible, isn't it?

A: Sure. That's fine. Our apple pie is quite good.

B: I think _____ to try something different today.

Do you have peach pie?

A: Yes, we do. It's also very good.

Conversation 3

A: Look! Those cookies look delicious!

B: They sure do. I'm sure the children would love those chocolate

ones, but they eat so much chocolate. _____

get those plain cookies. They look good, too.

A: If you have the coupon from the newspaper, you can get fifty

cents off a box. Why don't you buy two or three boxes?

B: _____ have so many cookies around the house.

I'm trying to lose weight and so is George.

Look at the three conversations again.

Which takes place in a grocery store?   Conversation _____

Which takes place in a restaurant?   Conversation _____

Which takes place in someone's home?   Conversation _____

7 *VOCABULARY*

Complete the sentences with the correct form of *do* or *make*.

❶ We all hate _____ *doing* _____ the housework, especially _____ *making* _____

the beds.

❷ Mrs. Robinson _____ the best lemonade I've ever tasted.

❸ I didn't have time to _____ my homework last night.

❹ Your living room looks great! You _____ a good job

decorating it.

❺ We're going to _____ hamburgers and hotdogs on the

barbecue tonight.

❻ His favorite hobby is _____ model airplanes.

❼ The washing machine isn't working right so we didn't _____

the laundry today.

❽ Sam has been talking behind his sister's back. He's always

_____ trouble for her.

8 *WRITING*

**Read Carol's answer to Chris' letter (on page 44 of your textbook).
Find ten mistakes and correct them.**

Dear Chris,

Please forgive me for not writing sooner. I was really embarrassing to hear that it has been over a year since I wrote. I'd rather not to give a lot of excuses. Just believe me when I say I've been very busy. Work is OK, I guess. Sometimes it's interesting and challenging, but sometimes it's really bored. I often think I'd rather be at school that to be here. Living away from home isn't easy. I have to do everything myself when I get home from work: make the shopping, do the housework, and make the laundry. I really don't make anything in my free time because I don't have any.

I don't want this letter to sound depressing! There are some good things about my job, too. I'm learning a lot about advertising even though I'm just a receptionist here. One of my company's ads published in a big sports magazine last month. I'm sending you a copy. Do you like it?

Believe it or not, I've become very interesting in vegetarian food. My favorite dish is Green Bean Jamboree. It invented by a friend of mine. You'd love it. Why don't you come to visit some weekend and I can make it for you. I'd really like to see you again.

Love,

Carol

❶ <u>"Embarrassing" should be "embarrassed."</u>

❷

❸

❹

❺

❻

❼

❽

❾

❿

TEST 1

Circle the most appropriate answer *a*, *b*, or *c*.

1 He _____ here until next weekend.
   a   has been staying
   b   is staying
   c   stayed

2 Mrs. Erwin promised _____ the boys to the zoo.
   a   taking
   b   take
   c   to take

3 We're all looking forward to _____ on vacation.
   a   going
   b   go
   c   be going

4 What are you thinking _____ tonight?
   a   to do
   b   about doing
   c   in doing

5 Try to avoid _____ fattening foods.
   a   eat
   b   to eat
   c   eating

6 _____ me help you?
   a   Will you let
   b   Will you need
   c   Will you like

7 I think it _____ tomorrow.
   a   is raining
   b   is going to rain
   c   rains

8 How much money _____ so far this month?
   a   did you save
   b   have you saved
   c   had you saved

9 Mike's changed a lot, _____?
   a   isn't he
   b   hasn't he
   c   has he

10 Would you mind _____ the door, please?
   a   close
   b   to close
   c   closing

11 When the alarm clock _____, I got up.
   a   was going off
   b   went off
   c   goes off

12 He's tall and handsome, _____ a movie star.
   a   like
   b   as
   c   similar

13 John and Meg have known _____ for one year.
   a   themselves
   b   each other
   c   the other

14 I _____ to the Art Museum twice this month.
   a   went
   b   have been
   c   was going

15 I don't smoke. I _____ last year.
   a   gave it up
   b   gave it back
   c   turned it off

16 He _____ when he had the accident.
   a   drove
   b   was driving
   c   used to drive

17 We all wished him a lot of _____.
   a   success
   b   successful
   c   succeed

18 John's a wonderful guy. He's easygoing and _____.
  a kind
  b snobbish
  c rude

19 My husband prefers fish _____ meat.
  a than
  b more than
  c to

20 I prefer going to a disco _____ to the movies.
  a go
  b going
  c to going

21 _____ students applied for a scholarship last year.
  a Less
  b Only a few
  c Only a little

22 I'm up to my _____ in work.
  a ears
  b feet
  c heart

23 _____ people went to the lecture.
  a Only a few
  b Only a little
  c A lot

24 _____ I used to get up early.
  a When I go to school,
  b When I went to school,
  c Now

25 It was a very exciting _____.
  a competition
  b competitor
  c compete

26 That wool blanket _____ by my aunt.
  a made
  b was made
  c has been made

27 We were _____ after the three-hour hike.
  a exhausted
  b exhausting
  c exhaust

28 Mr. and Mrs. Lee were embarrassed _____ their son's behavior.
  a for
  b by
  c in

29 Harry would rather work nights _____ days.
  a to
  b than
  c for

30 _____ your homework last night?
  a Did you make
  b Did you do
  c Have you done

1 *LANGUAGE STUDY*

The Past Perfect and the Simple Past

A **Use the pairs of verbs correctly to complete the following sentences.**

❶ *went / had gone*

After I _____ to the library,

I _____ home.

❷ *ate / had eaten*

I _____ only potatoes

and vegetables for dinner because my brother

_____ all the meat.

❸ *had / had had*

Mary _____ a bad night's sleep

because she _____ too much to eat

at dinner.

❹ *bought / had already bought*

When I got to the store someone _____

the last pair of boots on sale in my size, so I

_____ a pair of shoes instead.

B **Complete the sentences with the Past Perfect**
(*I'd been / I hadn't been*).

❶ I (*make*) __***hadn't made***__ a reservation before going to the

Riviera Restaurant so I had to wait for a table.

❷ By the time I sat down to eat, I (*lose*) _____ my appetite.

❸ It didn't take long to recover it when I saw the delicious food

the chef (*prepare*) _____.

❹ Most of the people (*leave*) _____ before I finished eating.

❺ I (*be*) _____ to the Riviera Restaurant before,

but I'll definitely go again.

**C Complete the sentences with the
verb in the Simple Past or Past Perfect.**

When Pearson National Bank

[1](*call*) _____

Paul for an interview early Monday morning,

he was a little surprised. He

[2](*answer*) _____

their ad for a security guard a month before and

[3](*not hear*) _____

anything since then. When Paul

[4](*receive*) _____

the call, he [5](*feel*) _____

a little nervous. He [6](*take*) _____

a long, relaxing bath and

[7](*put on*) _____

the suit he [8](*buy*) _____

for his high school graduation in June.

Paul [9](*write*) _____

hundreds of letters in the last few weeks, but

this [10](*be*) _____

the first reply. Most places were looking for people who [11](*finish*) _____

college. Paul really [12](*need*) _____ this job.

He [13](*not save*) _____ enough money to go to college full time and his

parents couldn't help him very much. A few days earlier he [14](*receive*) _____

a letter saying that he [15](*be accepted*) _____ into the State College's

evening program starting in September. If he got the job at Pearson National Bank he could work during

the day and go to the State College in the evenings.

D Look at the sentences, and circle *he'd* when it means *he had*.

1 He'd be happy if they gave him a job.

2 He'd answered a lot of different ads.

3 He'd decided to go to school in the evenings.

4 He'd have to find time to study.

What does the other *he'd* mean? _____

2 *WHAT ABOUT YOU?*

1 When you started studying English, had you already learned another language?

_____

2 Had you met any of the other students in your class before you started studying with them?

_____

3 Had you already decided what you wanted to be when you were ten years old?

_____

3 *LANGUAGE STUDY*

Impersonal they

Make the sentences more informal by using *they*.

1 A public swimming pool has been built in our neighborhood.
  They've built a public swimming pool in our neighborhood.

2 It was opened to the public yesterday.

_____

3 Lifeguards are needed for this summer.

_____

4 Season tickets will be sold at a cheaper price.

_____

5 Hundreds of children are expected this weekend.

_____

6 Free T-shirts will be given to the first 50 visitors.

_____

4 LANGUAGE STUDY

The Causative: Having Things Done

A Choose the best completion for each sentence.

❶ Edward should be a mechanic. You know, (**a** *he fixed his motorcycle himself.* | **b** *he had his motorcycle fixed.*)

❷ Bobby looks awful with his hair so messy. I'm really glad (**a** *he's cutting it this afternoon.* | **b** *he's having it cut this afternoon.*)

❸ My car is so dirty. Maybe I'll stop by the automatic car wash this afternoon and (**a** *wash it.* | **b** *have it washed.*)

❹ Doesn't the kitchen look great! My husband and a friend (**a** *painted it last weekend.* | **b** *had it painted last weekend.*)

❺ One of Billy's teeth has been giving him a lot of trouble, but he doesn't want to (**a** *pull it out.* | **b** *have it pulled.*)

B Complete the conversation. Use *had* and the correct form of the verb in parentheses.

A: Emily, you look so different. What did you do to your hair?

B: I ¹(*dye*) _____. It's the newest color.

It's called "Flame Red."

A: And your nose? It looks smaller. Is that possible?

B. I really hated my old nose so I ²(*fix*) _____.

A: And your fingernails are just perfect. I've never seen such beautiful nails.

B: Thanks. I've always had nice nails, but I ³(*polish*) _____

yesterday at the beauty parlor.

A: Wow! What a change! And your dress is fantastic. Where did you get it?

B: Actually, I didn't buy it in a store. I ⁴(*make*) _____.

5 WHAT ABOUT YOU?

Complete the questions. Then answer them.

❶ Do you ever cut your hair or do you ___have it cut___ ?

___I always have it cut.___

❷ If you had a lot of money, would you build your own house or would you _____ ?

_____

❸ Have you ever taken a family picture or have you _____ ?

_____

❹ Does someone in your family clean the house or do you _____ ?

_____

6 VOCABULARY

Underline the correct words.

A: Did you know I started a new ¹(*job* / *work*) last month?

B: No, I didn't. I thought you were happy where you were before.

A: I was, but the ²(*salary* / *pension*) wasn't very good, and I wasn't able to ³(*save* / *spend*) much at all. I got tired of working the night ⁴(*turn* / *shift*), too. Now I'm working days and I like it much better.

B: Well, I'm glad to hear that. What kind of ⁵(*prizes* / *benefits*) do you get?

A: They're pretty good. We get free medical insurance and a four-week vacation.

B: That sounds good.

A: Yeah! And I ⁶(*earn* / *win*) $50 more a week. With the way the ⁷(*price* / *cost*) of living is going up, that extra money will sure help.

B: I bet it will. By the way, now that you're going to be a rich man, do you think you could ⁸(*lend* / *borrow*) me $10 until Saturday?

7 WRITING

**Read the diary entry and fill in the blanks to make logical sentences.
Then use your imagination and complete the entry.**

Dear Diary,
Today I got up on the wrong side of
the bed! It seems as if everything went
wrong. I got up late and by the time I
reached the bus stop, my bus _____
_____. I had to walk to school.
Classes had already started when

UNIT 7

1 VOCABULARY

Complete the crossword. Numbers 1, 3, 5, 6 and 8 are synonyms of *intelligent*. The other words are opposites. If necessary, look at page 56 of your textbook for help.

2 LANGUAGE STUDY

The Definite Article the

A Look at the pairs of sentences. Decide which one needs the definite article, and write it in the blank.

❶ a _____ children of high intelligence often prefer to associate with older children.

b _____ children who attend the new experimental school are very intelligent.

❷ a _____ parents of gifted children have to be careful when selecting a school.

b _____ parents should choose their children's school carefully.

❸ a Many gifted children have a good ear for _____ music.

b _____ music written by Mozart at a very young age is a good example of this.

B Read the article. Cross out the word *the* where it is used incorrectly.

Rebecca Strong was *the* youngest graduate at S.W. State College yesterday. She is only 17 years old. Rebecca majored in *the* marine biology, something which has fascinated her since she was very young. "I started reading *the* books about *the* sea animals at a very early age, and I've always been fascinated by *the* sea," she says. Rebecca hopes to find a job doing *the* laboratory work this summer.

Rebecca's interests are not limited to *the* science. She also has a great love for *the* music and plays *the* violin quite well. When asked about her plans for *the* fall, Rebecca said, "I would like to continue studying and eventually get my Ph.D. *The* education is *the* most important thing for me right now."

3 *LANGUAGE STUDY*

Adverbs and Expressions of Frequency

A Underline the adverb of frequency which best completes the sentence.

Working nights isn't [1](*sometimes* / *often*) easy. It [2](*frequently* / *never*) forces people to make adjustments in their daily routine. It [3](*usually* / *seldom*) takes them a while to get used to sleeping during the day, especially if noise bothers them. Some people may even have to take sleeping pills [4](*now and then* / *constantly*). Night workers [5](*rarely* / *frequently*) spend their mornings like most people do; when almost everybody is getting up, they are [6](*usually* / *never*) going to bed. Fortunately, after working a night shift over a period of time, they [7](*usually* / *hardly ever*) have problems.

B **Write sentences by putting the adverbs in the correct place.**

❶ (*frequently*) I have problems sleeping during the day.

_____

❷ (*usually*) Any kind of noise keeps me awake.

_____

❸ (*once in a while*) Fortunately, I only work nights.

_____

❹ (*rarely*) I have fallen asleep on the job.

_____

❺ (*never*) I can use public transportation to go to work.

_____

❻ (*always*) The buses stop running before I have to leave for work.

_____

❼ (*hardly ever*) When I work nights, I sleep more than six hours.

_____

4 *WHAT ABOUT YOU?*

Answer the questions using an adverb or expression of frequency.

❶ How often do you watch movies in English?

_____

❷ How often do you speak English when you're not in school?

_____

❸ How often do you do your homework with a friend?

_____

5 LANGUAGE STUDY

Relative Clauses with who, which, *and* that

**A Complete the sentences with *who, which,* or *that*.
Some sentences have two possible answers.**

❶ When Thomas Edison got bad grades, his mother, _____ was a teacher, took him out of school and taught him herself.

❷ The only job _____ Einstein could get when he graduated from college was in the Swiss patent office. His job, _____ was to write descriptions of new inventions, helped him to write more clearly.

❸ Leonardo da Vinci, _____ lived almost 500 years ago, left drawings of many different inventions. The descriptions of the inventions _____ he drew had to be read with a mirror because they were written backwards.

❹ Mozart is probably the composer _____ wrote music at the youngest age.

❺ Ung Yong Kim, _____ was born in Korea in 1963, spoke Korean, German, English, and Japanese when he was four years old.

B Join the following sentences. Use *who*, *which*, or *that*.

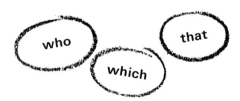

❶ Ed Allen is an excellent carpenter. He never had any formal education.

Ed Allen, who is an excellent carpenter, never had any formal education.

❷ Ed used comic books to teach himself how to read. He still has those comic books.

❸ Ed wanted his son to get a good education. He was never able to get one.

❹ Ed's son goes to a private school. It's one of the best in town.

❺ The school has a special program for adults, too. It has a very good reputation.

❻ Ed has always wanted to learn more. He is thinking of taking some classes.

6 WHAT ABOUT YOU?

Complete the questions with the superlative of the adjectives. Then answer the questions.

❶ What is (*good*) _____the best_____ book you've ever read?

_____

❷ What is (*interesting*) _____ subject you are studying now?

_____

❸ Who is (*tall*) _____ person you know?

_____

❹ What is (*exciting*) _____ vacation you can imagine?

_____

❺ Who do you think is (*pretty*) _____ actress in your country?

_____

7 VOCABULARY

A Make a new word from each word given. Use –er, –or, or –ist and make any necessary changes.

❶ type _____   ❻ photograph _____

❷ collect _____   ❼ reception _____

❸ compose _____   ❽ psychiatry _____

❹ invent _____   ❾ pharmacy _____

❺ speak _____   ❿ philosophy _____

B   Read the paragraphs. Then rewrite the sentences which complain about something. Use *always* and the Progressive.

❶   The students in my class are well-behaved. They're polite and they get along well with each other. The only problem is that they arrive late to class. A few of them forget to bring their books, too.

_____

_____

❷   We like most of our teachers at school. They really want us to learn and they're interested in us. We don't mind doing homework during the week. But they give us a lot of homework on weekends and we can't stand that. We think that we should have weekends free to spend time with our friends or do whatever we want.

_____

_____

8   *WRITING*

Read the description of Bennett School. Find eight mistakes and correct them.

The children from all over the country study here at Bennett School. We are one of the few boarding schools in this area. Our campus, that is located five kilometers from the nearer city, provides a quiet, relaxing environment for the student.

Our academic program is one of the goodest in the country. Each student is carefully interviewed before selecting his or her program of classes.

Besides our academic program, we offer all kinds of sports and free time activities: the horseback riding, basketball, baseball, football, the swimming, and many more.

The school hardly ever provides visits to museums and cultural centers because we feel this is an important part of a child's education.

If you are interested in visiting the school, please call and make an appointment. We are rarely happy to show you our facilities.

UNIT 8

1 LANGUAGE STUDY

The Conditional in Present Hypothetical Situations

A Draw lines to make four logical sentences.

❶ If he had his bathing suit

❷ If he went swimming

❸ He'd go swimming

❹ He'd be cooler

a if he went swimming.

b he'd go swimming.

c he wouldn't go alone.

d if the water weren't so cold.

B Complete the sentences with the following verbs. Use each verb only once.

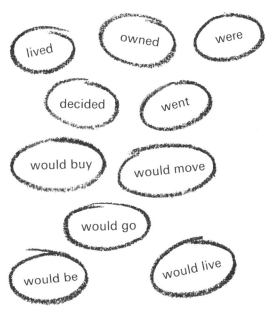

If I ¹_____ to move to the country, I ²_____

near a river. If I ³_____ near a river, I ⁴_____ a small

boat. If I ⁵_____ a small boat, I ⁶_____

fishing every day. If I ⁷_____ fishing every day, I

⁸_____ bored. If I ⁹_____ bored, I

¹⁰_____ to the city again.

C Complete the questions and answers as in the examples.

❶ (do / win) What _would you do if you won_____
a lot of money?

❷ (buy) _____I'd buy_____ a yacht.

❸ (go / own) Where _____
a yacht?

❹ (sail) _____
to a small island in the Pacific.

❺ (eat / live) What _____
on a small island?

❻ (have) _____
a lot of fish and fresh fruit.

❼ (do / be) What _____
lonely and bored?

❽ (return) _____
to the United States.

D Write questions for the answers given below.

❶ Q: _What would you do if you didn't have to work today?_____

A: I'd probably read a good book.

❷ Q: _____

A: I'd probably wear my green dress.

❸ Q: _____

A: I'd talk to them nicely and ask them not to make so much noise after midnight.

❹ Q: _____

A: I'd go to the embassy and apply for another one.

❺ Q: _____

A: I'd buy a motorcycle and take a long vacation.

❻ Q: _____

A: I'd probably call the police.

2 *WHAT ABOUT YOU?*

Complete the sentences with information about yourself.

❶ If I had more time, _____

_____

❷ I'd speak English better _____

_____

❸ If I were rich, _____

_____

❹ I'd be happier _____

_____

3 *LANGUAGE STUDY*

Giving Advice with should (not) *and* ought (not) to

A Draw a line to match each problem with the appropriate advice.

❶ I can't see very well with the glasses I'm wearing.

❷ I don't seem to have any energy in the morning.

❸ I really need to get some exercise, but I can't seem to find the time.

❹ The doctor says my blood pressure is very high.

❺ My kids are having problems with their teeth because they're always eating cookies and candy.

a You should try walking to work.

b You should have your eyes checked again.

c You shouldn't eat such salty food all the time.

d You ought not to buy so many sweets. If you don't have them, they won't eat them.

e You ought to have a good breakfast.

B Complete each sentence with *should* or *shouldn't* and one of the following verbs:

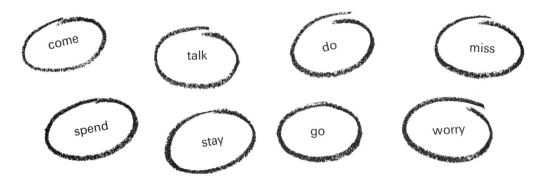

come   talk   do   miss   spend   stay   go   worry

A: I'd really like to go to the beach for a week or so, but Henry thinks we

1_____ _____ home. What 2_____

I _____? I'm tired of spending my vacations at home.

B: You 3_____ _____ to Henry about it. I'm sure

he'll understand.

A: I've tried, but he won't change his mind. He just hates the beach. He refuses to go.

Besides, he says we 4_____ _____ money on a vacation

when we could use it on other things.

B: Then I think you 5_____ _____ alone. There are some

really inexpensive trips that include plane, hotel, and a week on the beach.

A: I know, but what about Henry?

B: You 6_____ _____ about him. I'm sure he'd love to have

a few days by himself. You 7_____ _____

this opportunity.

A: Maybe you're right. You know, you 8_____ _____

with me. A little sun would be good for you, too.

B: Now that you mention it, maybe I will.

4 *WHAT ABOUT YOU?*

❶ Do you think that a family should always go on vacation together?

_____

❷ Do you think that parents should let their teenage children go on vacation with their friends?

_____

5 *VOCABULARY*

A   Complete the conversation with the following expressions:

to be very fond of

to envy

can't stand

to be crazy about

to get on (somebody's) nerves

A: Sometimes my Aunt Sally [1]_____. She's always

repeating the same thing over and over again.

B: I know. That's something I [2]_____ either. One

of my best friends does it all the time. I guess they don't realize it.

A: You're right. Aunt Sally has always been very good to me. Actually, I

[3]_____ her. We have a lot in common.

B: Oh really?

A: Yeah! We both adore Charlie Chaplin movies. We [4]_____

him. Aunt Sally, Uncle Bill, and I go see a lot of his old movies together.

B: I [5]_____ you. I don't have any relatives at all in town. I

wish I did.

B   Underline the correct words.

Susan was [1](*delighted* / *fascinated*) when she received a phone call from Margaret, her best friend who lived 1,000 miles away. She still remembered how [2](*furious* / *depressed*) she had felt when Margaret had told her about her husband's transfer. Then, Susan had promised to write every month. Susan felt [3](*astonished* / *embarrassed*) as she thought about this; her last letter had been sent over five months ago. Susan felt sorry [4](*for* / *with*) Margaret. Moving to a small town after living in a big city wasn't easy. Margaret was [5](*bored* / *boring*) and [6](*lonely* / *delighted*). As soon as she heard Margaret's voice, she realized she was worried [7](*about* / *with*) something. Margaret told her how her husband had changed since they moved. He wasn't interested [8](*in* / *on*) anything anymore, not even his work. He was jealous [9](*with* / *of*) her and her new friends. At first, Margaret had suspected he was [10](*at* / *in*) love [11](*with* / *about*) another woman, but that wasn't the case. He just acted differently. Susan was [12](*astonished* / *terrified*) when she heard this. John had always seemed to be such a well-balanced person. She wondered what she could do to help.

6   WRITING

Write a letter to a foreign friend who is coming to your country for a year to study and wants advice.

Tell your friend what schools in your country are like.
Tell your friend what he / she should do before coming.
Tell your friend what he / she should or shouldn't bring.
Tell your friend about different housing possibilities.
Say what you would do if you were your friend.

_____

_____

_____

_____

_____

_____

_____

_____

_____

_____

_____

UNIT 9

1 LANGUAGE STUDY

Can *and* be able to

A Draw lines to make four correct sentences.

❶ She is able to speak English

❷ She was able to speak French well

❸ She'll be able to speak some German

❹ She would be able to speak more Italian

a if she studied more.

b quite well now.

c when she lived in Paris.

d when she finishes the intensive course.

B Rewrite the underlined verbs with a form of *be able to*.

A: [1]Can you sleep well at night now that you have a baby?

B: Oh, yes. Becky is a wonderful baby. I get at least six or seven hours of sleep every night. If I went to bed earlier, I [2]could sleep even longer. My problem is I'm used to staying up late so I [3]can never get to bed before midnight.

A: You're lucky she lets you sleep. When Timmy was smaller, I [4]couldn't sleep much at all. I was always tired. By the way, do you think you [5]can come to Timmy's party next Saturday? He's going to be five.

B: What time?

A: About five o'clock. There won't be too many kids. A lot of them are on vacation so they [6]can't come. Timmy's best friends will be there, though.

B: Sure. We'd love to come.

❶ _____

❷ _____

❸ _____

❹ _____

❺ _____

❻ _____

C Complete the sentences with *can* or *will be able to*. Some sentences have two possible answers.

1 _____ you _____ go to the movies with us tonight?

2 _____ I _____ borrow your car next week?

3 She _____ say a few words in Japanese after her first lesson.

4 He _____ not _____ hear if he doesn't have

an operation.

5 The baby _____ walk in a few months.

6 We _____ move to our new house by the end of the month.

Which sentences cannot be written with *can*? _____

2 LANGUAGE STUDY

Unless *vs.* if

A Choose the correct meaning.

1 He won't go unless it's sunny.
- **a** If it's sunny he'll go.
- **b** If it's sunny he won't go.

2 If his car is still in the garage, he'll take the bus.
- **a** He won't go by bus unless his car is in the garage.
- **b** He won't go by car unless it's in the garage.

3 His girlfriend will go unless she has to work.
- **a** His girlfriend won't go unless she has to work.
- **b** His girlfriend won't go if she has to work.

B   Read the ad and then complete each sentence with _if_ or _unless_.

Young Adults Skiing Group

- Only for experienced skiers (16 or over).
- We go on skiing trips every weekend during the winter months.
- Our bus leaves every Saturday morning at 8 a.m. from North East Bus Terminal and returns late Sunday afternoon.
- Hotel reservations must be made in advance, so please confirm by Friday morning by calling 734–8876.

1 _____ you haven't gone skiing before, you can't go with the group.

2 You can't go on the skiing trips _____ you are at least sixteen years old.

3 _____ you want to stay in the hotel, you must reserve a room.

4 _____ you want to return Sunday morning, you can't take the bus.

5 You'll miss the bus _____ you get to the terminal by 8 a.m.

6 You can't join the group _____ you're not free on weekends.

---

3 _LANGUAGE STUDY_

The Conditional in Possible (What will happen if …?)
and Hypothetical (What would happen if …?) _Situations_

A   Make six logical sentences.

_____ **1** She'll be 100

_____ **2** She'd live in a home for the elderly

_____ **3** She won't retire at 65

_____ **4** She'll go to live in a home for the elderly

_____ **5** She would be astonished at today's society

_____ **6** She'd continue working for ten more years

a if her health is good.

b if she were alive.

c if she didn't have so many other interests.

d if there were one near here.

e if they build one soon.

f if she lives for three more years.

B Complete the conversation with the verbs in parentheses in the correct tense.

James: At what age would you like to retire?

Tim: Well, I really enjoy my work. If my health ¹(*be*)_____ good

when I ²(*be*)_____ 65, I ³(*continue*)_____

working. Of course, if I ⁴(*have*)_____ a

different kind of job that required a lot of physical work, I

⁵(*retire*)_____ earlier. It all depends on each

individual, on the kind of job you do, and on your health.

James: What do you think you ⁶(*do*)_____ when you

retire?

Tim: I think I ⁷(*take*)_____ a long trip. I've always

wanted to visit Japan. Some of my friends are also interested in

visiting the Far East. So, unless something terrible

⁸(*happen*)_____, that's our plan.

4 *WHAT ABOUT YOU?*

❶ What do you think you'll do in your free time when you retire?

_____

❷ Would you continue working if you were 65 but had very good health?

_____

❸ If you were very rich, would you stop working at an early age?

_____

5 LANGUAGE STUDY

The Simple Future (will do) *vs. the Future Progressive* (will be doing)

A   Choose the best answer for each question.

① Would you like to go to a seven o'clock movie this evening?

   a   Thanks, but I can't. I'll pack my suitcases.

   b   Thanks, but I can't. I'll be packing my suitcases.

② Where are you going?

   a   On vacation. Tomorrow at this time, we'll visit Montreal.

   b   On vacation. Tomorrow at this time, we'll be visiting Montreal.

③ If you leave at eight o'clock where will you be at lunchtime?

   a   We'll drive through Canada.

   b   We'll be driving through Canada.

④ What will you do when you get to Montreal?

   a   We'll look for a hotel.

   b   We'll be looking for a hotel.

B   Look at the pictures and answer the questions using the Future Progressive.

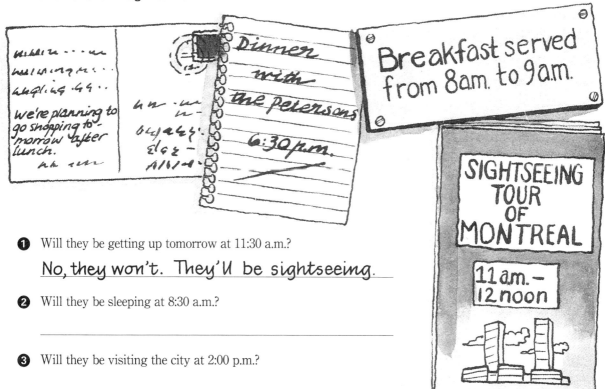

① Will they be getting up tomorrow at 11:30 a.m.?

<u>No, they won't. They'll be sightseeing.</u>

② Will they be sleeping at 8:30 a.m.?

_____

③ Will they be visiting the city at 2:00 p.m.?

_____

④ Will they be shopping at 7:30 p.m.?

_____

C Complete the letter with the verbs in parentheses.
Use the Future or Future Progressive.

Dear Cousin Paul,

I'm writing to let you know that a couple of my college friends and I ¹(travel)_____ around France the last two weeks in June. ²(work) _____ you _____ then? If not, maybe you can come along. I'm sure we ³(have)_____ a wonderful time. Mary wanted to come too, but she's getting married on August 1st and she ⁴(get ready)_____ for the wedding. She'd really like you and Aunt Michelle to come if you can.

Mom and Dad are fine. Dad ⁵(retire)_____ on September 30th when he turns sixty-five. He's bought a small house in the country and as soon as the old house is sold, they ⁶(move)_____. They're really excited about that... especially Dad! You know how much he likes country life!

We haven't gotten our plane tickets yet, but as soon as we do, I ⁷(let you know)_____ the exact date of our arrival. I can't wait to see you! Write soon. I ⁸(wait)_____ to hear from you.

Your cousin, Mike

6 WHAT ABOUT YOU?

❶ Do you think you'll be studying English five years from now?

_____

❷ Where do you think you'll be living in the year 2002?

_____

❸ Next year, will you still be doing what you do now?

_____

7 WRITING

Look at the letter in Exercise 5C. Imagine you are Paul and answer your cousin's letter.

Dear Mike,

    I got your letter telling me about your trip to France. I'm sorry, but I won't be able to travel with you in June because (*give a reason*) _____
_____.

Do you think you might be able to change the dates of your trip? (*say when you would be able to go*) _____
_____.

    I was happy to hear about Mary's wedding. I think we'll be able to go unless (*say under what circumstances you won't be able to go*) _____
_____.

    I still remember when Mary was 9 years old and spent the summer with us. I remember she (*say something she wasn't able to do well when she arrived*) _____
_____, but

by the end of the summer she (*say what she was able to do very well*) _____.

    Say "hi" to your mom and dad for me. (*say you are happy about his retirement*) _____
_____.

    Write when you have more definite plans about your trip.

                 Love,

                 Paul

E STUDY

could *vs.* should (ought to)

ld, should (ought to), or *might* to complete each sentence correctly.

❶ You (*could / might*) go on the nature trip with the school only if you have your parents' permission.

❷ You (*shouldn't / might not*) walk alone in the woods or you (*should / might*) get lost.

❸ You (*could / should*) extinguish all your cigarettes carefully when you are camping or you (*might / should*) start a fire.

❹ Some people are careless and leave empty cans and garbage around. They (*might / ought to*) be more considerate.

B   Complete the sentences with *might*, *should*, or *could*.

A: I've been studying hard all week. I ¹_____ really get away this weekend and relax. Have you made any plans?

B: Fred and I ²_____ go camping, but we're not sure. If we do, would you like to come?

A: I'd love to. We ³_____ use my new tent. I bought it three months ago and I haven't had a chance to use it yet. It sleeps three.

B: Great! That's all I needed to hear to help me make up my mind. Let's see. I think we ⁴_____ leave on Friday afternoon, if that's OK with you.

A: That's fine with me. We ⁵_____ go in my car if you like.

B: I don't know. Fred ⁶_____ want to take his. It's a little bigger, I think. We probably ⁷_____ call him and make sure he's still interested.

A: You're right. Let's call now. We ⁸_____ not wait too long or he ⁹_____ make other plans.

C **Read the situation and then add a comment using**
might, could, **or** *should.*

1 Fred has never slept in a tent before.

   He might not like sleeping in one.

2 They're not sure if they will be able to catch any fish in the river.

_____

3 The weather forecaster says the temperatures will drop about ten degrees this weekend.

_____

4 Fred wants to take his new car, but he doesn't have any car insurance yet.

_____

5 It hasn't rained for several months and there have been a couple of fires in the area lately.

_____

6 It's a long drive. It will take them about eight hours to get there.

_____

2 *WHAT ABOUT YOU?*

1 What do you think you should take on a camping trip?

_____

2 What are some problems you might have if you've never been camping before?

_____

3 What kind of food would you take with you if you went camping for a weekend?

_____

4 What could you do if you got lost in the woods?

_____

3 *LANGUAGE STUDY*

Past Modals: might (may) have done *and* could have done

A   Use a Past Modal and the verb in parentheses to complete the newspaper article.

Three Youths Disappear on Camping Trip

Three teenagers who were last seen camping near the Valley River have disappeared. No one seems to know what happened to them. One camper said, "I saw them swimming early Saturday morning. They seemed to be good swimmers, but they [1] (*could / drown*) _____ _____. The river is known for being very dangerous." When our news reporter talked to the parents of one of the boys, they said, "We think the boys [2] (*might / get lost*) _____ _____. They didn't know the area well. We're hoping the search party will find them safe and sound." Some campers speculate that the teenagers [3] (*may / have*) _____ _____ an accident and be in need of help. Others, who are more optimistic, say that the boys [4] (*may / run out of*) _____ _____ gas on one of the country roads on their way home. A number of things [5] (*could / happen*) _____. The Valley search party has been working since sunrise and hopes to find the boys before nightfall.

B   Read the situations and then write one possible explanation.
Use *might have (done), may have (done),* or *could have (done).*

1 The Wilsons usually keep their dog in the backyard, but I haven't seen it for several days.

_____

2 Mrs. Lee has been looking all over the house, but she can't find her umbrella.

_____

3 The police stopped at my neighbor's house yesterday.

_____

4 Mr. Dodd had a dentist's appointment yesterday afternoon, but he never showed up.

_____

5 Billy started crying in the middle of the night.

_____

6 My brother told me he'd be home by five o'clock. It's six o'clock and he hasn't arrived yet.

_____

4 VOCABULARY

Form nouns from the following words. Then write them in the correct column. Use your dictionary if necessary.

explode	describe	provide	revise	perform
concentrate	destroy	appear	imagine	decide
disappear	operate	divide	tolerate	insure

explosion	*concentration*	*disappearance*

5 VOCABULARY

Fill in the blanks with *reason*, *cause*, or *purpose*.

A: You're home from work early. Why? Aren't you feeling well?

B: I feel fine. The ¹_____ I'm home early is that all the

lights went out in the downtown area. They still don't know what the

²_____ was.

A: Really! So they told you to go home?

B: Well, actually, I suggested it. What would be the ³_____

of sitting around doing nothing when I could be using the computer

here?

A: That's true! And they don't know what the ⁴_____ of

the blackout was?

B: They suspect it might have had something to do with the new lines that

are being put up.

6 LANGUAGE STUDY

Expressing purpose with (in order) to *and* so (that)

A Complete the sentences in the most logical way.

1 The WWF began in 1961 in order to _____

2 Operation Tiger was started in order to _____

3 The WWF wanted to make a film about tigers in India in order to _____

4 A wildlife film crew went to India so that _____

5 The cameramen had to keep themselves and their equipment out of sight so that _____

6 When people saw the film on television, they sent money to the WWF in order to _____

a the tigers were not frightened away.

b protect all threatened wild animals and plants.

c save more wild animals in the future.

d save the tiger population in India.

e they could film the tigers in their natural environment.

f make the general public aware of threats to wildlife.

B Complete the following sentences with (*in order*) *to*, *for*, or *so* (*that*).

1 _____ be a wildlife cameraman, a person needs a lot of patience.

2 They have to try to be in the right place at the right time _____ they can get good films of the animals.

3 These cameramen don't work principally _____ money because the financial rewards are very small.

4 Wildlife cameramen film _____ the joy of being out in the open and near wild animals.

5 _____ make a good film they have to travel to far off places.

C Fill in the blanks with *for* or *to*. Then use each phrase to complete one of the sentences.

HOW MUCH DO YOU KNOW ABOUT ANIMALS?

a _____ air

b _____ fly

c _____ defense and communication

d _____ survive

e _____ wash its face and ears

f _____ pump blood all the way to its head

g _____ food for the family

1 The bat uses a type of radar _____ .

2 Many types of fish produce "sounds" _____ .

3 The female lion or lioness is the one who goes hunting _____
_____ .

4 The giraffe's heart, which is enormous, needs a lot of force _____
_____ .

5 Baby hippopotamuses are born under the water, but they come to the surface from time to time
_____ air.

6 The okapi has a very long tongue which it uses _____ .

7 Koala bears have a very special diet. They need to eat the leaves of eucalyptus trees _____
_____ .

7 *WRITING*

You and your sister made arrangements to meet a friend in front of a movie theater at 5:30 p.m. It's almost 6:00 p.m. and your friend still hasn't arrived. The movie is going to begin in a few minutes. Write the conversation you have with your sister. Use some of these phrases:

Do you think we ought to ... ?

We should(n't) ...

Why do you think ... ?

He / She could have ... *or* He / She might have ...

... so we won't miss the movie.

... to find out what happened.

_____

_____

_____

_____

_____

_____

_____

_____

_____

TEST 2

Circle the most appropriate answer *a*, *b*, or *c*.

1 The robbers _____ when the police arrived.
  a already left
  b had already left
  c used to leave

2 I think I'm going to make an appointment to _____ tomorrow.
  a have cut my hair
  b have my hair cut
  c cut my hair

3 Gregory is one of _____ students in his class.
  a smart
  b smarter
  c the smartest

4 Ed Jones, _____ was the best soccer player at Center High, plans to play professionally.
  a who
  b which
  c that

5 George _____ me 20 dollars last week.
  a borrowed
  b lent
  c earned

6 I don't like TV so I _____ watch it.
  a constantly
  b hardly ever
  c once in a while

7 Nobody knows the secret to _____.
  a happiness
  b the happiness
  c be the happiest

8 The people _____ in line want to talk to the director.
  a who are
  b who is
  c whom are

9 He'd like to become a _____.
  a chemistry
  b chemist
  c chemical

10 What would you do if you _____ in an elevator?
  a are trapped
  b were trapped
  c would be trapped

11 My teacher thinks I _____ study more.
  a should
  b ought
  c must

12 You're going to come to the concert with us, _____?
  a will you
  b won't you
  c aren't you

13 If you drove faster, we _____ get home before dark.
  a will be able to
  b can
  c would be able to

14 I was _____ when I saw Mary walking down the street with my boyfriend.
  a fascinated
  b furious
  c terrified

15 He wants to _____ speak English by the end of the year.
  a can
  b be able to
  c know

16 I'll die of hunger _____ I eat soon.
   a if
   b unless
   c although

17 Do you know what you'll be doing when you _____ 65?
   a will be
   b are
   c would be

18 By this time next year, he _____ in his father's law firm.
   a will work
   b will be working
   c is going to work

19 We're not sure, but we _____ go out for a pizza later.
   a must
   b might
   c could

20 If you want to see *Macbeth* you _____ get your tickets early.
   a should
   b must
   c might

21 You _____ tired! You didn't even hear the alarm clock.
   a might have been
   b must have been
   c should have been

22 He gave a detailed _____ of the criminal.
   a describing
   b description
   c describe

23 The _____ I need a loan is to help pay for a new car.
   a reason
   b cause
   c purpose

24 Elephants are killed _____ their ivory tusks.
   a so
   b in order to
   c for

25 They turned off the radio _____ he could study.
   a so that
   b in order
   c for

New Dimensions Intermediate,
Workbook

Copyright © 1993 by Longman Publishing Group

Longman, 10 Bank Street, White Plains, N.Y. 10606

Associated companies:
Longman Group UK Ltd., London
Longman Cheshire Pty., Melbourne
Longman Paul Pty., Auckland
Copp Clark Pitman, Toronto

Distributed in the United Kingdom by Longman Group UK Ltd.,
Longman House, Burnt Mill, Harlow, Essex CM20 2JE, England
and by associated companies, branches, and representatives
throughout the world.

ISBN: 0-8013-0851-8

1 2 3 4 5 6 7 8 9 10-AL-96959493